D1444374

SandCastle 1

Homophones

Harry is Not Hairy

Pam Scheunemann

ABDO Publishing Company

Published by SandCastle™, an imprint of ABDO Publishing Company, 4940 Viking Drive, Edina, Minnesota 55435.

Printed in the United States.

Photo credits: Comstock, Digital Vision, Eyewire Images, Image State, John Foxx Images, PhotoDisc, Rubberball Productions

Library of Congress Cataloging-in-Publication Data

Scheunemann, Pam, 1955–
    Harry is not hairy / Pam Scheunemann.
      p. cm. -- (Homophones)
    Includes index.
    Summary: Photographs and simple text introduce homophones, words that sound alike but are spelled differently and have different meanings.
    ISBN 1-57765-743-8
    1. English language--Homonyms--Juvenile literature. [1. English language--Homonyms.] I. Title. II. Series.

PE1595 .S36 2002
428.1--dc21

                                                                                    2001053315

The SandCastle concept, content, and reading method have been reviewed and approved by a national advisory board including literacy specialists, librarians, elementary school teachers, early childhood education professionals, and parents.

Let Us Know

After reading the book, SandCastle would like you to tell us your stories about reading. What is your favorite page? Was there something hard that you needed help with? Share the ups and downs of learning to read. We want to hear from you! To get posted on the ABDO Publishing Company Web site, send us email at:

sandcastle@abdopub.com

About SandCastle™

Nonfiction books for the beginning reader

- Basic concepts of phonics are incorporated with integrated language methods of reading instruction. Most words are short, and phrases, letter sounds, and word sounds are repeated.

- Book levels are based on the ATOS™ for Books formula. Other considerations for readability include the number of words in each sentence, the number of characters in each word, and word lists based on curriculum frameworks.

- Full-color photography reinforces word meanings and concepts.

- "Words I Can Read" list at the end of each book teaches basic elements of grammar, helps the reader recognize the words in the text, and builds vocabulary.

- Reading levels are indicated by the number of flags on the castle.

SandCastle uses the following definitions for this series:

- Homographs: words that are spelled the same but sound different and have different meanings. *Easy memory tip: "-graph"= same look*

- Homonyms: words that are spelled and sound the same but have different meanings. *Easy memory tip: "-nym"= same name*

- Homophones: words that sound alike but are spelled differently and have different meanings. *Easy memory tip: "-phone"= sound alike*

Look for more SandCastle books in these three reading levels:

Level 1 (one flag)	**Level 2** (two flags)	**Level 3** (three flags)
Grades Pre-K to K 5 or fewer words per page	**Grades K to 1** 5 to 10 words per page	**Grades 1 to 2** 10 to 15 words per page

Note: Some pages in this book contain more than five words in order to more clearly convey the concept of the book.

hair   hare

Homophones are words that sound alike but are spelled differently and have different meanings.

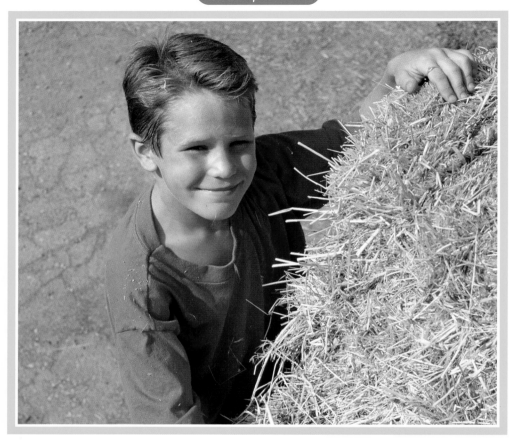

Mike stands by the **hay**.

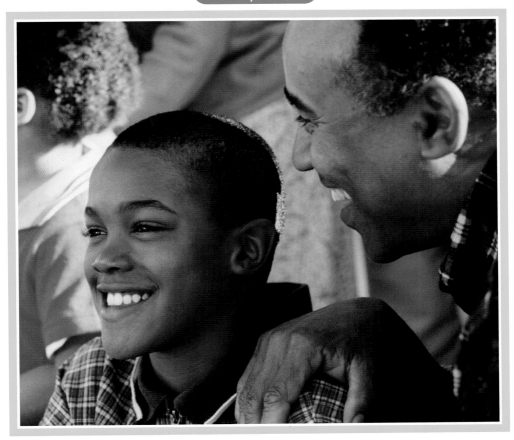

Hey Dad. This is fun.

The girls **heard** a joke.

Horses run in a herd.

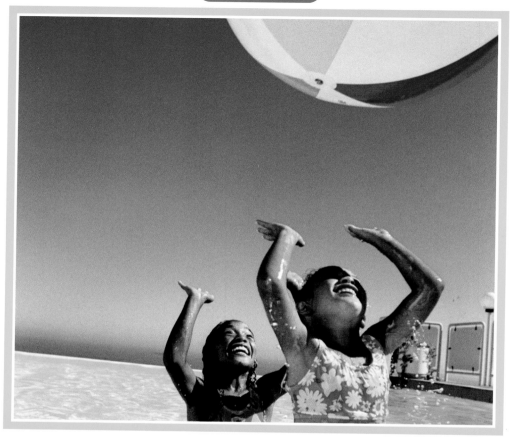

They threw the ball
higher.

We did not hire help.

The ball is near the **hole**.

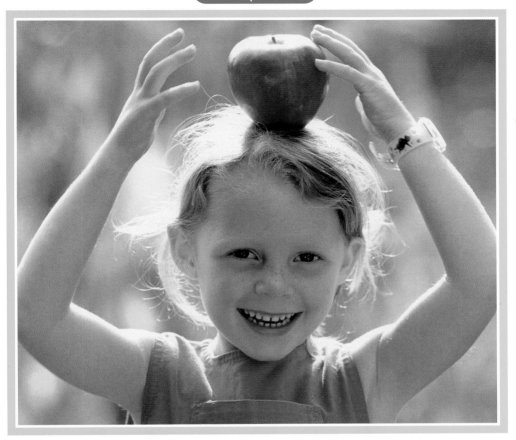

Andi has a whole apple.

Jill played for an **hour**.

Our family trip is fun.

Doctors help us **heal**.

This heel is raised.

Ann says **hi** to Spike.

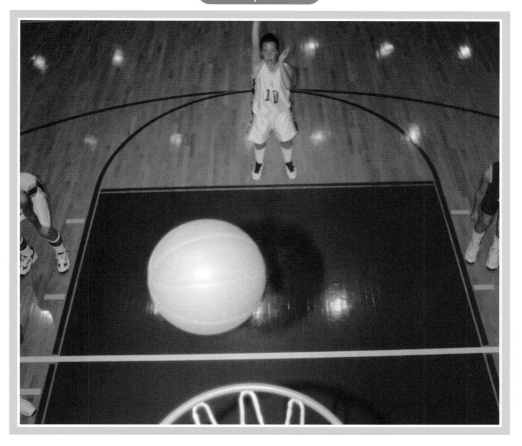

Tracy threw the ball high.

Grandpa **hoes** the garden.

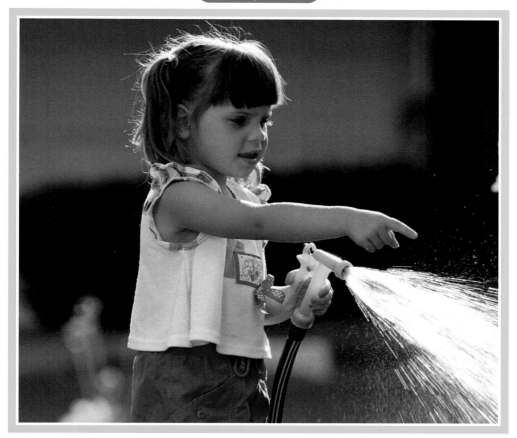

What does Amy water
with?

(a hose)

Words I Can Read

Nouns

A noun is a person, place, or thing

apple (AP-uhl) p. 13

ball (BAWL)
pp. 10, 12, 19

doctors (DOK-turz)
p. 16

garden (GARD-uhn)
p. 20

girls (GURLZ) p. 8

hair (HAIR) p. 4

hare (HAIR) p. 4

hay (HAY) p. 6

heel (HEEL) p. 17

herd (HURD) p. 9

help (HELP) p. 11

hole (HOHL) p. 12

homophones
(HOME-uh-fonez)
p. 5

horses (HORSS-ez)
p. 9

hose (HOHZ) p. 21

hour (OUR) p. 14

joke (JOKE) p. 8

meanings
(MEE-ningz) p. 5

trip (TRIP) p. 15

words (WURDZ) p. 5

Proper Nouns

A proper noun is the name
of a person, place, or thing

Amy (AY-mee) p. 21   Jill (JIL) p. 14

Andi (AN-dee) p. 13   Mike (MIKE) p. 6

Ann (AN) p. 18   Spike (SPIKE) p. 18

Dad (DAD) p. 7   Tracy (TRAYSS-ee)

Grandpa   p. 19

     (GRAND-pah) p. 20

Verbs

A verb is an action or being word

are (AR) p. 5   is (IZ) pp. 7, 12, 15, 17

did (DID) p. 11   played (PLAYD) p. 14

does (DUHZ) p. 21   run (RUHN) p. 9

has (HAZ) p. 13   says (SAYZ) p. 18

have (HAV) p. 5   sound (SOUND) p. 5

heal (HEEL) p. 16   spelled (SPELD) p. 5

heard (HURD) p. 8   stands (STANDZ) p. 6

help (HELP) p. 16   threw (THROO)

hire (HIRE) p. 11   pp. 10, 19

hoes (HOHZ) p. 20   water (WAW-tur) p. 21

Picture Words

hole

whole

hose

hoes